BRITACULUS™

VERY
LONG(ING)

BRITACULUS

For ma.
For as long as there is now,
I'm going to try my best
to get you out of
the projects.

CONTENTS

Long Suffering

"whether with a lover
or
none.
i reek of love.
i stink of love."

-Nayyirah Waheed
Nejma

Climb my mountaintop.
Reach its peak.
Let it move you to praise God.

I wonder if the loneliness
that strokes you to sleep each night
whispers my name.

I don't ask for much
all I want is
your last name.

I don't care for jewelry.
I just want a diamond ring.

Take me to a private lagoon
with a trickling waterfall.
Nowhere loud or boisterous.
I want it to fall gently
so that I can hear the echoes of creation
breathing life into each other.
Take my hand.
Guide me to the waters.
Show me the depths of the coral reefs.
Teach me to breathe underwater.

-honeymoon

Believe me.
I'm trying hard to swim
towards your bait.
But it seems that
you are mesmerized
by the colors of all the
other fish in the sea.

I want to give you a son.
I want to create someone just like you.
So that someone, somewhere
will also know what this feels like.

Frankly, it's a blessing
that you are there and I am here.
Because selfishly,
I know you would spin me in a web
that I would desperately
want to get stuck in.
You might suck the life out of me
and I might enjoy
every moment of it.

We all have that one thing
we resort to in order to ease the pain.
I just pray yours isn't as harmful.

Even if it splits me in half
and cuts me at every angle,
I want to love
the whole way through.

She heard his voice
through the lines of poetry
and felt him
through the pages of her books.
So descriptive was her imagination
that she could taste the sweetness of his lips
and smell the satiating splendor
that would feed her debilitating hunger.

But she never saw him in real life.

I can be as delicate as a flower
if you promise to work like a bee.
Watch my petals bloom
right before your eyes.

Some of us are just intensely aware
each time our hearts fall flat.
And the desperation comes in
at the desire to revive it
just to keep it beating –
however faint it may be.
No, we are not desperately looking for love,
we're looking for Aspirin
to buy us more time
in the hopes of breathing again.

-flatline

I am a slave of love looking for my freedom.
I am a slave held in bondage
praying for emancipation.
I am also that slave
in fear of the day
when the bells of freedom ring.

I'm searching for sights and smells.
Anything that reminds me of you.

I want to go to Euphoria.
A place far away
where no one sees
but you and me.
Where we can touch
tender feelings
and not worry about
who is going to find out.
I want to look into your eyes.
I won't blink out of fear
of missing a single moment in time.
Let those tears run down your sweet cheeks.
Let it stay there unabashedly.
You are my weakness
and I need to tap into you
under no false pretense.
Unify my feeble bones.
As I've been broken and far too long alone.
Take this journey with me.
Love me tenderly.

Unrestrained love
without limits.
Picture that.

This touch,
this feeling
does not belong to me.
This dream
that cannot be mine.
But to feel your caress
and to taste your kiss
is the sweetest little sin
I could ever find myself in.

Tell me how
the weight of the world
feels upon your shoulders.
Let me carry it with you.

Dive into my ocean.
Take long concentrated strides.
Come up for air
only when necessary.

Right now,
I choose
not to speak words of
self-love and self-reliance.
I need you.
I'm throwing my entire
body and soul
on the line.
Accept my vulnerability
as I spill my emotions to you
in absolute humility.

Do not trample on my heart.
I can submit
and I can summit.
You choose which way
we're going to go.

Tell me the names of all your scars
and how deeply they sink into your skin.
Tell me how much it pains your heart
and if it's forever embedded in your mind.
Even the ones that have faded away,
do you remember their names?

Long Story Short

"You know, Francie, a lot of people would think that these stories that you're making up all the time were terrible lies because they are not the truth as people see the truth. In the future, when something comes up, you tell exactly how it happened but write down for yourself the way you think it should have happened. Tell the truth and write the story. Then you won't get mixed up."

-Betty Smith
A Tree Grows in Brooklyn

I'm just going to sit here
and let this thing fester.
I'm going to let it grow all over
and within me
until it eats me alive.
I will allow the thought of you
to overtake me
like mold growing through
the walls of my protected heart.
I'm not fighting this living thing anymore.
Work your way from the inside out
so that when you are good and done,
the existence of me
will be confused with the existence of you.
They will ask me where I've gone
and I will say that
I've traveled to a destination
where I've sacrificed my soul
unto you.

One day you will step into your skin
and you will finally feel
how safe you are there.
You will feel the warmth of home
and it will be hard
to ever let that feeling go.

This morning I am waking up
to the sound of the rain.
The world is still fast asleep.
Lightning strikes
as my phone simultaneously
alerts me of the flash flooding in my area.
But all I can feel
is purity through the chaos.
Let's go out in the rain and dance.
Let the storm sweep us away.
And when we've laughed ourselves silly,
let's slowly peel our wet garments off
and saturate the earth
our own special way.

i

There's a ladder to heaven
that I'm trying to climb.
Everyday I work tirelessly to get closer.
At sunset, I rest on the clouds.
I lay on my back and watch the colors
in the sky change from
orange to pink with shades of purple.
I give silent praise for His majesty.
I feel small and insignificant in comparison.
Yet, somehow, I'm reminded of my worth
as the stars start to twinkle and shine
in my favor.
They sing me to sleep
and whisper sweet things into my ears.
I feel safe.
I am not alone.
I look at the comfort surrounding me.
I sleep soundly knowing I am loved.

ii

At dawn, when it's time for the clouds
to fall and feed the earth
with its morning dew,
that's when I continue my journey.
Some days are harder than others.
But my nights are always the same.

We're always looking for more.
Sometimes I think that just maybe,
we'll never be satisfied.
Because once we get more,
we want a little bit extra.
And once we get extra,
there's still yet another thing
we haven't achieved.
And if "less is more",
is it healthy to stop striving for more
and just accept the least
you have in front of you?

There's this thing that I know is real.
A thing that is out there.
I've heard reports
and I've seen the conviction
in their eyes.
Some are afraid of it.
Some run to it recklessly.
And some will never know it.
But it's there.
Lingering.
Wanting.
Pulsating.
Hoping.

i

I stood at the intersection of
Oxford Circus and Regent Street
with tears in my eyes
and all of my emotions stuck in my throat.
I told everyone I loved
that I'd see them soon.
I lied.
Unless there is some profound calling
that brings me back,
I will not step foot on the Queen's soil
again because third times a charm
and I've always known
that four-leaf clovers
have nothing to do with my destiny.
It all boils down to the realization that
as much as I'd like to
make a place or people my home,
sometimes home is not
where you're desperate to make it.

ii

Sometimes home is right there
in the uncomfortable situation
that builds up your character.
Home is within
the makings of your own heart.
And once your heart settles to
a rhythm that's steady
and you no longer need
jolts of defibrillation,
you can then settle down
and find home
anywhere in the world.

-London

I hope to always remember
moments like this.
Sitting in this Dairy Queen in Union Square
eating your emotions
with flies flying all around you
and you can't move because
this germ-infested couch is comfortable
and it takes too much energy to get up.
Nonetheless, you're grateful.
Because the cashier gave you free fries
and that was the kindest thing
anyone has done for you
in a long time.

If the future is really female,
that's going to be weird.
We need our men.
Being feminine for ourselves
and amongst each other
is like dancing salsa with your girlfriends.
Yeah, it's fun and all,
but there's nothing like
his one hand resting on your waist
and the other directing your movements
with the gentle nudges
and pressure from the tips of his fingers.
And yes, we can all dance solo,
but how breathtaking it is
to see synchronized harmony
when everyone moves naturally
to the beat of the music.

-harmonize

If I had a choice to live or to die,
I think the truth would hurt
so, I'd rather lie.
To love or not at all
What is life if you never fall?
How would you know
the heights and the depths
if you've never had anyone
take away your breath?
Your existence will touch
just the surface of life.
Your feelings would be basic,
no light revealing that sacred glow
in your eyes.

My cave is overrun by bats
and draped in cobwebs.
The writings on my interior walls
tell of my untold story; my ancient past.
And the deeper you travel with questions,
the darker the answers.
But I invite you to turn my light on.
Strike a flame.
Trace your fingers around
truths hidden in dirt.
Figure me out; read my hieroglyphics.
Complete the story for me.
Tell them how I lived
and how you saved me.
Then embed our prints into rocks
so that the world never forgets
how we invented our own love story
and how you made yourself home
in an abandoned cave.

Please don't live your life like New York City trains by allowing people in and out as they please. They will run to you like you are the only one in the world that will lead them to their destination. They will pry their fingers into you to keep you open as long as possible to delay your personal progression. And once they're in, they will spit on your walls. They push where it hurts and will give no kind consideration to your time and the weight that you carry pacing back and forth because you are a person of loyalty.

So, when you tell them to stand clear, use your strength of steel to shut them out. And should you decide that they are welcomed inside, make sure you tell them not to lean on your doors while you are in steady motion because the next stop will be the last stop with no free transfers if they do not stand on their own two feet.

I am the autumn tree
that changes through the seasons.
When it gets too cold for me,
I will lay my soul bare.
I will blossom only when I feel warm.
And though I change with the seasons,
I am faithful.
I am rooted where I stand.
My foundation is set for centuries to come.

i

What if the universe disrespected us
the way we disrespect it?
What if gravity no longer
wanted to hold us down?
What if the moon rebelled
and no longer wanted to reflect
the light of the sun
desiring to leave us in darkness?
How would you feel if the clouds
decided to shower us with
carbon monoxide instead of rain?
…or if the trees wanted to choke us
from existence
and spewed nitrogen into our air?
Would it be fair if mountains
used their power against us
and bullied us into slave-like submission?
…gauged our eyeballs like gold miners
and penetrated our atmosphere,
raping our ozone layer?

ii

What if it took from us
what we take from it?
It sounds absurd
for our wonderful God-given home
to overstep its purpose
in such drastic ways.
And just maybe,
we've overstepped ours.

It's always exciting when
things start brewing.
When the kettle whistles
you know that it's time for
coffee or passion
or whatever is bubbling within.
You might burn your tongue
because it's just so hard
to resist the heat
flaring up into your nostrils
awakening your entire
mind and body,
taking you places
you could never get to
without your morning latte,
tea or kiss.
And you can have it any way you like it.
Sweet with cream,
dark and strong,
smooth with multiple shots of espresso…

The nights are silent
but it rings a cry of hope.
Somehow through much anticipation
and holding on,
dawn breaks,
dew sets and
life begins again.

-never give up

You will know the moment you realize
that one explanation
is all it takes.
There will be less questions
and more understanding.
And once you are accepted
for who you genuinely are,
that's exactly when you'll know.

The very longing of you
brought me closer to her.
All those quiet nights
wrestling the sheets of my bed
as if I were unworthy
of the care and attention
I desperately craved.
It birthed hatred into my understanding.
It screwed up my face
into a distant gaze.
We stayed domestically violent
until I looked into the mirror one day.
The girl staring back at me
had dark groping eyes.
She was silently reaching for my attention.
So, I decided to respond.
We've become lovers.
We spend time together
and we're learning to respect the process.
She found that you were never the answer.
That it was me
she was looking for all along.

There are galaxies within
that will pull you deeper inside.
You will float your way into a black hole.
You have to grab hold of yourself
before it's too late.
Chase the shooting stars.
Let the speed of light wake you.
And pray for gravity!
Let Heaven know that you
wanted to get lifted.
That you compromised at Orion's Belt.
That the Big and Little Dippers
were nothing to be mesmerized by.
That Mars came with the heat of red.
That the craters of the moon
made you stumble.
That the stars look beautiful
but they burn.
And that Earth is the only place
where you belong.

Long Winded

"...don't hold your tongue.
You have the right to air out both your
lungs."

-George The Poet
Kids

To me,
you are a diamond
that shines
in the heat of pressure.

To them,
you are the elements of rust
that just sits there,
festering.

i

I realize it becomes a problem
when they ask you
how you really feel.
What they should say is:

Tell me what I want to hear.

Because then I will decorate my
words the way they like to hear them.
I will say all the things
that makes them smile and
makes their heads nod in approval.
But if I am asked how I feel,
I will tell them how much it hurts.
I will splatter the pool of emotions
plaguing my heart
like the last bit of blood
draining from my cold lifeless body.
The knots gagging my throat
will excrete like vomit into their faces.

ii

Maybe I am to blame
for allowing this sickening spell
to terrorize my thoughts and actions.
But I am a prisoner to my truth.

So please think twice
before deciding what you want to hear
when you ask me
how I really feel.

Don't pity my words.
I am introducing myself to you
in the hopes that my exposure
produces a sense of community.
We are all muddling in the same dirt.
Yours might be dry
and mine is mostly wet.
But we can wipe each other clean
with a little bit of tender compassion.

Their smiles are
plastic and recycled.
You can call it what you want,
it's still garbage.

In the game of chess,
the King just sits in his protected castle
moving as little as possible.
His Queen fights his war
taking on bishops and knights.
She is the most prominent player
in his kingdom
as she glides across the board
in any direction she pleases
to protect her man.
And his only goal is to pretend to
make moves
just so nobody can step to him,
on his domain,
and check him.

-boy, bye

You placed me on a timeout in a corner far away from you so that I would learn my place in your life. You came back wondering if I learned my lesson and told me exactly where you thought I'd be of use in your world. I'm not sure if you knew who you were dealing with. But I sat, not in the corner you designated, I went to another. I looked within. I learned my place quickly. I stood up and slipped my pride back on.

When you came back with your demeaning smile offering me false opportunities, I stopped you in mid sentence. I handed you my insecurities, walked past you and never looked back.

-fool me once

Ask me a question
but don't question me.

-intentions

I don't want to talk about
the things of the world.
I want to talk about us.
The world gets complicated
with its protests and speeches.
I want to talk about love.

If it gets too complicated,
all I ask for are your arms
to wrap around me as we
rock from side to side,
with our quivering hearts skipping beats
and your fingers
sliding up and down my spine
like a bass guitarist
trying to keep a tune together.

We know we appear to be lost.
But in reality,
we know exactly where we want to be.
We just don't know how
we're going to get there.

I'm not angry.
I simply have a lot of pain.

They don't realize
that strong people break too.
We are the shattered mosaics
that people stare at in amazement.
We decorate the windows of holy places.
We are fragmentally pieced together
because we have no other choice.
We wish to sit comfortably on easels
and have someone stroke our pretty faces
into something wonderfully artistic.
Instead, we gather ourselves from the dirt
and secure our hearts piece by piece.
But they watch the colors
and stones that glisten in our eyes.
They praise our crystal tears as they fall.
Shimmering down trails left behind
from all the tears that we've shed before.
The salt feels like pain to our open wounds
and their amazement threatens to
shatter us even more.

Most would confuse my candid speech
with pessimism.
But let's face it,
look at how we treat each other.
Look at the world.
I have no reason to sugarcoat anything.

There is no more sweetness in my blood.
Mosquitoes wouldn't even take a bite.

I'm afraid to say
that this sadness
is becoming a permanent part
of our personalities.

You were never happy for me.
Every joy I felt
was received as a challenge to compete.
So, I finally realized how it had to be.
I would drift away
like a friend suddenly lost at sea.
You might wonder where I've gone
but in the end, you will agree.
Our shallow waters
will be calm
as we find depth within ourselves.
And the further I take myself away,
the more we'll find
that inner peace.

-drifting away

When circumstances change
and we try to soften the blow,
we promise that it's not going to be
the last time we'll see each other.
We extend invitations
saying they'll always have a place
to visit.
But the truth is that
we probably won't see them again.
They will become someone
that we knew from somewhere.
And as time goes on,
we'll slowly forget
who they were entirely.

You don't ever have to worry about
fighting with me.
I will always excuse myself.
I know hostility.
He made his presence known
when he should have felt like home.
Don't worry about winning or losing,
I will always walk away
from the heat of fire.

I'm not old schooled
or conservative.
I'm just consistent.
I don't need to change course
with everyone else.
Left is left.
Right is right.
I'm not into all the squiggles and loops.
All that spinning
makes me nauseous anyway.

-popular opinions

I cannot allow myself
to live vicariously through you.
But I promise
to be happy for you.

I've moved on,
I haven't forgiven.
What does that say to you?

Go ahead,
dissect my feelings
like a frog in biology.

-I didn't think it was that serious

We have more knowledge than
we have ever had before.
But we are more sad,
more lonely.
If knowledge has been the power,
why do we still feel defeated?

My defenses rise
when my personality
gets attacked
and when you slap a label on it
saying my reaction is
a product of my
stereotypical nature,
as if I am not privy
to feel.

Our gentlemen
are becoming gentle boys.

Our scared little girls
are becoming intimidating women.

It wasn't a question of whether
she still had it.
It was a question of
if she ever had any at all.

You can't tell me that we've grown apart
when you've given up in your efforts
to grow together.
I understand that people change,
but it takes both of us
to yield to the needs of each other
with respect and acceptance
of who we are individually
and who we're becoming.
If any one of us lets that go,
the bonds that keeps us together will break,
sending us in opposite directions.
So, if we're growing apart,
we are to blame
for giving up on each other.
But don't make me believe
it's because we suddenly had
different ideas
when one or both of us
just gave up.

Don't do it
for the sake of conversation.
Half of everyone
is lying anyway.

Sometimes the cause of death
isn't what happened immediately
before one takes their last breath.
Sometimes it's the silent killers like
heartbreak or low self-esteem
that goes unchecked
and spreads violently,
consuming a person to the point of feeling
unworthy to even try to fix it.

-don't let yourself go

The heat of my passion
has turned all the way up
to the fire of my fury.
How else does a flame burn
without stimulation?
Except to grow into
something massive,
finding anything to burn
to keep it alive
and catastrophic.
You sparked my imagination
and flickered a light.
I grew wild,
panting for air.
But you stopped,
dropped and rolled
your way out of my life
while I've been here,
raging on.

I can no longer
draw conclusions of you
with paper and pen
for I have finally
run out of ink.

Watch how the birds
start singing a different tune
when the rest of the flock
comes to the nest
and begin laying their eggs
next to yours.

-ideologies

They beat us into a mold
and shove their philosophies
down our necks.
We are then made to believe
the lies we are told.

What if at the end of it all
you turn out to be a moth
instead of a butterfly?

-at least you still have wings

Belong

*"It doesn't matter who's in front of us when
we remember who's behind us"*

-Unknown

1936.
As the years pass by,
I fear one day
I won't hear her shaky voice
on the other side of the phone.

-my one and only

It's not about the child support.
It's about supporting the child.

I've never raised a child,
but I was one.
I know how it feels.
I've never been married,
but I know divorce.
I know how it feels.

-torn

My expectations for men are high
because a village of women raised me.
There wasn't a single thing
they couldn't do.
But they spoke of their loneliness
come nighttime.
I have grown accustomed
to this conversation
and I wonder if we will ever
speak about anything else.

Divorce is something we know well.
We carry it around like birthmarks
written in the fabrics of our skin.
I am determined to change this anomaly
by nursing the scars of love
so that they become less visible.

You have taught me everything
I need to know about men
from your silent lectures
and your phantom appearances.

Men, please understand
the power you have in our lives.
Your presence,
makes us women feel more secure.
It gives our sons something to look up to
and our daughters the self-confidence
to love themselves.
Your existence in our lives
shapes our future
and solidifies our families.

I want to be involved in the lives
of all the people with missing teeth
that smile like they have
everything they need in the world.

*-to the Chinese woman that comes to the deli
at 242nd Street every morning*

Standing with my arms crossed
is not a subliminal message
that I'm closing you out.
I'm trying my best
to hold myself together.
If I let myself go,
will you piece me back in place?

i

Your amputated breast reminds me that you are more woman than a lot of us. And every time I look at your blackened skin where the radiation sizzled your flesh, I think of how heroic you were as it burned greater fear into your heart, as if you needed more heat in your life.

I remember kissing your bald head and saving the last strands of hair that you held onto for dear life. Like those few strands could save the nation of dying follicles lingering in your scalp. I remember that smile pretending to be okay. I remember every morning pretending to be brave. I remember holding you up as my faith fell to the ground. I remember swallowing that bitter taste of fear. I remember the heart attacks. I remember the party. I remember simultaneously learning to never surprise a heart patient. I remember your lips turning blue. I remember the cardiac arrest that followed and the resuscitation. I remember the coma and the doctors telling me to make

ii

a decision to "pull the plug". I remember
our friends and family. We would have
never made it without them.

We never talk about it, mama. I think we
were traumatized and reliving that time
brings painful memories. Sometimes I have
nightmares. But what I remember most is
the look on your face when you realized that
party was for you and you were surrounded
by the ones that love you most. I remember
the moment you woke up from that coma at
the sound of my voice calling you by your
pet name. I remember it all and I'm so
grateful to God that we still stand together
silently remembering.

-cancer

I want to be remembered
as the one who made you feel something.
When I return to the dirt,
remember me for all the times
I made you smile when it hurt
because that is the one time
I feel most alive.

If our cycles could sync
imagine what women could accomplish
if we allowed our hearts to blend.
We're more connected than we realize.

-elevate one another

My mom's hand is the one hand
I wish to hold onto forever.
From my first step to my first heartbreak.
To the first time I became a lady,
she has guided me every step of the way.

Her hand in mine
is the only one I dream of
as she walks me down the aisle
to give me away.
And when I'm clutching hers
on the day I give birth to my first child.

Her hand in mine
when sickness threatens our hold.
When the mind leaves
and our skin turns cold.

Her hand in mine is the only way
I want us to go.

Please just be happy for me.
It took me awhile to get here.

I'm sorry if my writings bore you.
I don't have a juicy story to tell.
All I can hand you is my heart.
Please return it to me gently.
Thank you for your patience.
I'll take it from here.

Longevity

*"Do unto others
as you would have them do unto you"*

-Golden Rule

Take your time
in your hugs and in your kisses.

i

If there's one thing I've learned
it's the importance of building.
Look at the people surrounding you.
That's your material,
work with it.
Build on love and respect
with each person in your life.
Speak to the hearts of the people
that makes your heart smile.
Go home to your spouses.
Tell them you love them.
Tell them what bothers you.
Speak to your friends.
Tell them you love them.
Tell them what bothers you.

Build.

ii

With each step we take,
we climb mountains.
We're reaching the peaks of life.
And when we make it to the top,
look at the landscape!
Look at all those
beautiful hearts you've touched
because you took the time to build.

-enjoy the climb, enjoy the view

Skin on skin contact is more important
than we realize.
It sends signals to the brain
telling a lover to give more or less.
It tells a doctor if someone has died.
It tells a premature infant to keep living.
It's what bonds us.
It's what speaks to others when
we're lost for words.

-never lose your touch

While you're trying hard
to justify why being with them
would make you happier,
really think about how much energy
they're putting into you.

Just make sure you're not
fighting so hard for someone
who isn't fighting just as hard
for you.

When you choose to walk around
with self-pity
and no one else in the world
gives it to you,
you have two choices:

You either become bitter
or you can look within
and change what you can change.

Your scars have always
been beautiful to me.
It tells me the story
you are too afraid to tell.
The marks on your face
tell me that you are from a different country,
tribe and village.
And that you have suffered your way
to a land of promises.

Your scars are beautiful.
And even if that wall gets built
and it cuts your wounds deeper
and rips your dreams to shreds,
carry your scars wherever you go
with honor
because it tells your story
even when you are silenced.

Angry people are only projecting
their fears and insecurities
onto you.

-misery loves company

Analyze your anger.
Is it really that one thing
that made you angry?
Or is your anger revealing
a subconscious emotion
of a real thing that seems to be lacking
or going unfulfilled in your life?

Just walk away.
Take your leave
and your dignity
and walk away.

Forgiveness is one thing,
but never forget.
Never forget how it
brought you to your knees.
Never forget how toxic it felt,
how empty it left you,
how cold it was.

Never forget so that you never go back,
but forgive yourself for it.
Let time heal your wounds.
Come back to yourself,
Forgive.
But never forget.

To be loved is one thing.
To be chosen is quite another.

Don't be upset with them
for not choosing to love you.
This is your thorn.
Don't prick others
with your bitter stems.
Uproot the negativity
from your tongue.
Let it bleed.
Let it heal.

Happiness is the outward manifestation
of an internal joy.
So, no matter what you do,
or where you go,
if you are not right within,
you will always be empty.
Work your way inside out.

May your goodness
be done in silence.

Your advice to people
sounds like noisy chatter
unless you are actually using it
to help someone.
People don't like to hear sermons.
They look for your physical hand
extending towards them.
They listen for messages on their phones.
They want your shoulder to cry on.
So, if you decide to use those fancy words,
do something that shows you mean it.

It's okay to be happy for people
at a distance.
There's no need to occupy spaces
that takes your peace away.

Trust the rhythm of your relationships.
If there's a disconnect,
you can try to level it.
But after awhile
it might be best to just
kill the music.

Most people are satisfied
with knowing the surface parts of you.
Be mindful of those who care
to dig a little deeper.

Whether you are an artist
that needs an audience,
or a child that needs a mother's love,
If you are a candidate running for office
and need votes,
If you are a plant desperate for water,
the truth is:
We all need each other.

If you're honest with yourself
I think you'll agree
that there were warning signs.
But in those moments,
you allowed the sound of your heart
to silence the logic
screaming the truth
in the quiet spaces of your mind.

If you're still talking about it,
it still bothers you.

Heartbreak comes in many facets.
It's not always the breakdown
of a romantic relationship.
Sometimes your heart breaks
as each disappointment slowly mounts
into a stiffened clogged artery.
It prevents the free flow
of vital juices that keeps us
fresh and vibrant.
It eventually deprives us of
the confidence we used to have
in one another.

Sometimes the attraction
is to the extent of boosting his ego
and nothing more.
So be careful the next time
you think there's a chemical reaction.
He might just be reacting from
an overdose of egotism.

You will hear all sorts of cautionary tales.
Appreciate the words that they speak.
But, live your life, darling.
You must learn your own lessons
and make your own mistakes.
Don't be afraid to breathe life
into your lungs.

The secret to life is balance.
Too much or too little is never good.
Apply that to every aspect of your life
and see what it does for you.
Push and pull.
Give and take.
Add and subtract.

There are benefits to being both
a sole proprietor
and having a partnership
in business and in life.
So be flexible
when it's time to change
and satisfy the supply and demands
of the various situations
you may find yourself in.

Forget being open minded.
Become open hearted.

Believe in your capabilities.
Believe in your mind.
Believe in your opinions.
Believe in your voice.

Once you believe in yourself,
people begin to believe in you.

Who we are is who
we allow ourselves to be.
You are better,
more beautiful,
more worthy
than what has happened to you.
It is not who you are.

-don't victimize yourself

It's very possible that
insecurity can turn into haughtiness.
Especially if you're elevating
something that makes you proud
and using it as a cover-up
to hide what's really lacking underneath.

-people who brag the most are concealing a
deeper pain

Shhh.
Stop shouting.
Everyone hears you.

Step back.
Breathe.

Whisper into silence.
They'll start asking
what happened
to all the noise.

-stop trying so hard to be heard

Take one day at a time.
You're doing well.

It's only in moments of solitude
that you truly get to understand
the meaning behind things.
In the shadows of fear
or in the heights of excitement,
it's only when you are alone with yourself
that your thoughts come together.
So, get to know yourself.
Make those uncomfortable silences
your closest companion
because at the end of each day,
and more dramatically,
at the end of it all,
all we really have,
is ourselves.

- END -

What makes my words worthy of being heard when there have been so many before me that have poured their hearts out on paper and pen?

Thank you from the bottom of my heart for giving me this chance. If at some point, I made you smile, thank you for your understanding. If my words made you frown, please know that my love is eternal, but our political correctness needs to strike a balance. We need to be free to express ourselves with respect and find comfort in our differences.

For those of you that have waited long in life, my prayer is that you never give up. I hope your longings get shorter and that you're using this long period of time to make yourselves better, not bitter. Your time will come.

I long to meet you all someday. Stay true to yourselves in the meantime. Stay genuine. Stay strong. Stay beautiful.

Made in the USA
Middletown, DE
21 September 2019